REVIVE ME
PRAYER
journal

A Journey to Refreshing Your Soul
and Renewing Your Faith

BRANDY WOODS-SMITH

TABLE OF CONTENTS

DEDICATION

This book is lovingly dedicated to the pillars of my life, whose support and love have been my unwavering foundation.

To my husband, Shawn Smith aka Suge, my rock and my protector. You support me without fail, love me unconditionally, and stands by me through every high and low. Your strength and love envelop me, making every challenge easy and every joy magnified.

To my cherished children, McKinzey, Madison, Shawndrika, Octavia, Shawn, and Sanya, I dedicate my prayers for your peace, protection, and the abundant blessings of God upon your lives. You are my heart's greatest treasure.

To my delightful grandbabies, the purest joy of my life, may you always know the depth of my love and the boundless joy you bring to every moment we share.

To my parents, Charles and Stephanie Hickombottom and Thomas Woods (deceased), my first teachers and believers. Your faith in me never wavered and your support has been my constant. Your belief in me has shaped the person I am today.

To my sister, Natalie Woods-West, who has stood steadfastly by my side through every twist and turn. Your unwavering support for all my endeavors and your enduring patience with my shenanigans have been a source of strength and laughter. Your presence in my life is a cherished gift, and this dedication would be incomplete without acknowledging the bond we share. Thank you for being not just a sister, but a true friend and confidant.

To my spiritual mentors, Pastor Johnny Henderson, Pastor Barbara Barrett, Bishop Dr. Connie Stewart, and Overseer Deliah Jones (decreased). Thank you for your guidance, wisdom, and the spiritual nourishment you've generously poured into my life.

To the communities that hold a special place in my heart – Childcare Millionaires Association (CMA), Traffic Sales Profit (TSP), New Life in Word, Ministries, and Life in Bloom – your fellowship and shared visions enrich my journey in ways words cannot express.

Above all, **I give thanks to God**, the author of all things, for the countless opportunities, blessings, and second chances. My heart overflows with gratitude for the grace that sustains me, the love that surrounds me, and the hope that guides me.

This journal is a testament to the collective love, faith, and support that have been my guiding lights. May it serve as a beacon of hope and renewal for all who journey through its pages.

Love,

Brandy Woods-Smith

Dear Cherished Reader,

As you embark on this journey of reflection and prayer, I want to extend my warmest welcome and heartfelt encouragement. This prayer journal is more than just a collection of words and prompts; it is a pathway to revival and a deeper connection with the divine power, will, and purpose for your life.

In the hustle and bustle of our daily lives, we often lose touch with the quiet, still voice within us that guides and sustains us. This journal is designed to be a sanctuary, a place where you can pause, reflect, and commune with God. It is here that you can lay down your burdens, celebrate your joys, and find the strength and wisdom to navigate life's complexities.

"The Lord is near to all who call on him, to all who call on him in truth." - Psalm 145:18. This scripture beautifully encapsulates the essence of this journal. It is an invitation to draw near to God, to seek His presence earnestly, and to discover His profound love and purpose for you

GOALS OF THE REVIVE US PRAYER JOURNAL:

- To revive your spirit, mind, and body in every aspect.
- To deepen your connection with God, understanding His power, will, and purpose for your life.
- To provide a space for reflection, gratitude, and spiritual growth.

HOW TO USE THE REVIVE US PRAYER JOURNAL:

- Approach each prompt with an open heart and mind. Let the scriptures guide your thoughts and prayers.
- You may choose to use this journal daily or a few times a week – the pace is entirely up to you. The goal is to complete the prayers and prompts in 100 days or less, but remember, this journey is yours, and there is grace in every step.
- Write freely and honestly. This is your personal space for expression and connection with God.
- Reflect on each prompt and scripture. Let them speak to you in your current circumstances, hopes, and dreams.

As you turn each page, my prayer for you is that you find renewal, peace, and clarity. May this journal be a tool that brings you closer to the heart of God, where you can experience His unending love and grace.

In His Service and With Love,

Brandy Woods-Smith

THE PURPOSE OF PRAYER

Prayer is the heartbeat of a vibrant spiritual life and an intimate conversation with God. It is in these sacred moments of prayer that we open our hearts to God, seeking His presence, guidance, and comfort. The purpose of prayer extends far beyond presenting our requests or expressing gratitude; it is about cultivating a relationship with our Creator, understanding His will, and aligning our lives with His divine plan.

Communion with God: At its core, prayer is about communion. It's a time to speak with God and, more importantly, to listen. In the stillness of prayer, we find a deep connection with God, where we can share our joys, sorrows, fears, and hopes. This communion nurtures our relationship with Him, making it more personal and profound.

Transformation: Prayer is transformative. It changes us from the inside out, shaping our hearts and minds to reflect God's love and grace. Through prayer, we invite God to work in our lives, guiding us toward spiritual growth and maturity. It's in the crucible of prayer that we are refined, our character is shaped, and our faith is strengthened.

Guidance and Wisdom: Life is filled with decisions and challenges that can often leave us feeling lost or overwhelmed. Prayer is the compass that guides us through these complexities. By seeking God's wisdom and direction in prayer, we are better equipped to navigate life's journey, making choices that honor Him and lead to true fulfillment.

Intercession: Prayer is also an act of love and intercession. When we pray for others, we are lifting them up before God, asking for His intervention and blessings in their lives. This selfless aspect of prayer reflects the heart of God, who calls us to love and care for one another.

Experiencing God's Presence: In the hustle of daily life, it's easy to feel isolated or disconnected from God. Prayer brings us into the awareness of God's constant presence. It reminds us that we are never alone, that God is with us in every moment, ready to offer His love, peace, and strength.

The Power of Prayer: Prayer is powerful. It has the ability to move mountains, heal the broken, and bring about change in our lives and the world around us. Through prayer, we tap into the infinite power of God, trusting in His ability to do immeasurably more than all we ask or imagine.

In this prayer journal, you are invited to explore the depth and breadth of prayer. Let each prompt guide you into deeper reflections and conversations with God. Remember, there is no right or wrong way to pray; what matters is that you come as you are, with an open heart and a willingness to engage with the Divine.

As you journey through these pages, may you discover the profound impact of prayer in your life. May it revive your spirit, deepen your connection with God, and reveal His power, will, and purpose for you.

THE POWER OF PRAYER

In the quiet moments of prayer, we touch something profound, something transcendent that connects us to the very essence of existence. Prayer is not just a ritual or a formula; it is the soul's sincere dialogue with God, a bridge between the human and the holy. The power of prayer lies not in the words we utter but in the openness of our hearts to receive, to be transformed, and to be led by a force greater than ourselves.

Transcending the Physical: Prayer elevates us beyond the confines of our physical reality, allowing us to tap into the spiritual realm where all things are possible. It's in this sacred space that miracles are birthed, where the laws of nature bow to the command of the Creator. The power of prayer lies in its ability to bring the supernatural into our natural world, manifesting healing, provision, and protection.

Inner Transformation: The true power of prayer is often most evident in the transformation it brings about within us. It molds our character, softens our hearts, and refines our desires, aligning them more closely with God's will. Through prayer, we gain the strength to forgive, the grace to love, and the humility to serve. It changes not just our circumstances but, more importantly, who we are.

A Source of Comfort and Peace: In times of turmoil and distress, prayer offers a sanctuary of peace, a haven where weary souls can find rest. It reassures us of God's presence and His unwavering love for us, reminding us that we are never alone, no matter the storms we face. The peace that prayer brings transcends human understanding, guarding our hearts and minds in chaos.

Fostering Connection: Prayer deepens our relationship with God, creating a bond that is intimate and personal. It's through prayer that we communicate with our Creator, expressing our deepest fears, our highest hopes, and our unspoken dreams. This divine dialogue nurtures our spiritual life, keeping our faith vibrant and alive.

Intercessory Power: The power of prayer extends beyond our personal needs, reaching into the lives of others around us. Through intercessory prayer, we become conduits of God's grace, channeling His love and mercy to those in need. It's a profound expression of love and solidarity, a testament to the belief that we are indeed our brother's keeper.

Catalyst for Change: Prayer is a powerful agent of change, both in our lives and in the world at large. It has the power to topple regimes, heal divisions, and bring about justice and righteousness. History is replete with stories of prayerful people who, through their faith and persistence in prayer, have brought about significant social and spiritual renewal.

As you engage with this journal, let each prompt invite you into a deeper experience of prayer. Approach it with expectation, knowing that you are engaging with a power that can alter the course of your life and impact the world around you. Let prayer be your constant companion, guiding you, transforming you, and empowering you to live a life of purpose and impact.

IMPORTANCE OF THE WORD OF GOD: READING, AFFIRMING, AND APPLYING THE WORD

The Word of God stands as the bedrock of our faith, a guiding light in a world that often seems shrouded in darkness. It is not merely a collection of ancient texts, but the living, breathing voice of God Himself, speaking directly into the intricacies of our lives. The importance of reading, affirming, and applying the Word of God cannot be overstated, for it is through these practices that we come to know the heart of God, understand His will, and live out His purposes for our lives.

Reading the Word:

- **Encounter with God:** Each time we open the Bible, we stand on holy ground. It's an encounter with the Divine, an opportunity to hear from God directly. Reading the Word invites God to speak into our situations, offering wisdom, correction, encouragement, and hope.
- **Spiritual Nourishment:** Just as our bodies require physical food for sustenance, our spirits thrive on the nourishment provided by the Word of God. It is our spiritual bread, essential for growth, strength, and vitality in our walk with God.

Affirming the Word:

- **Foundation of Truth:** In a world where truth is often relative, the Word of God provides an unchanging foundation. Affirming the Word means standing firm on its truths, letting it shape our beliefs, values, and convictions.
- **Weapon Against Deception:** The Bible is our sword in the spiritual battle, a defense against the lies and deceptions of the enemy. By affirming its truths, we protect our minds and hearts from being led astray.

Applying the Word:

- **Transformative Power:** Knowledge of the Word is not enough; its power is unleashed in application. Applying the Word to our lives means living out its teachings, letting it transform our thoughts, words, and actions.
- **Guidance for Living:** The Word of God is a lamp to our feet and a light to our path. It provides practical guidance for everyday living, offering principles for relationships, work, ethics, and more.

Integrating the Word into Daily Life:

- **Regular Reading:** Make reading the Bible a daily habit. Set aside a specific time and place for this spiritual discipline, approaching it with expectation and reverence.
- **Meditation and Memorization:** Meditate on the scriptures, pondering their meaning and relevance to your life. Memorizing key verses ensures that you have the Word readily available in every situation.
- **Practical Application:** Seek to apply the teachings of the Bible in real-life situations. Ask yourself, "How does this scripture apply to my current circumstances?" and "What is God asking me to do or change?"
- **Community Sharing:** Share insights and revelations from the Word with others. This not only encourages fellow believers but also helps to deepen your own understanding and application of the scriptures.

The Word of God is a precious gift, a treasure that holds the keys to living a life of purpose, fulfillment, and deep connection with God. As you engage with the Word, let it dwell in you richly, guiding your steps, transforming your heart, and equipping you to be a light in the world.

THE FORMULA FOR READING THE BIBLE IN A YEAR:

Divide by Days:

- There are roughly 365 days in a year. Divide the total number of Bible chapters (1,189) by 365 days. This gives you an average of about 3.26 chapters per day.

Mix Old and New Testaments:

- To keep your reading varied and maintain engagement, consider reading from both the Old and New Testaments each day. For example, you could read two chapters from the Old Testament and one from the New Testament daily.

Incorporate Psalms and Proverbs:

- Psalms and Proverbs offer wisdom and reflection that can be very enriching when read alongside other scriptures. Consider reading a Psalm or a section of Proverbs each day in addition to your other readings.

Plan for Catch-Up Days:

- Life can get busy, and you might miss a day or two. Plan for catch-up days by setting aside a day each month to make up for any missed readings. Alternatively, you could read a little extra each day to build in a buffer for busy times.

SAMPLE DAILY READING PLAN:

• Morning:

• 1 chapter from the Old Testament (starting from Genesis)

• 1 Psalm or a portion of a Psalm (starting from Psalm 1)

• Evening:

• 1 chapter from the New Testament (starting from Matthew)

• 1 section from Proverbs (starting from Proverbs 1, then cycle through as completed)

TIPS FOR SUCCESS:

• Use a Bible Reading App or Plan: Many apps and websites offer structured plans to guide you through reading the Bible in a year. These can provide daily reminders and track your progress.

• Journal Your Insights: Keep a journal of your thoughts, questions, and insights as you read. This can enhance your understanding and retention.

• Join a Group: Reading with others can provide motivation and accountability. Consider joining a Bible study group or starting one with friends.

• Pray Before Reading: Ask God for understanding and insight before you begin your daily reading. Prayer can open your heart and mind to the messages in the scriptures.

By following this formula and incorporating these tips, you'll be well on your way to successfully reading through the Bible in a year. Remember, the goal is not just to complete the reading but to deepen your understanding and relationship with God through His Word.

12-MONTH BIBLE READING PLAN:

This plan breaks down the Bible into more digestible sections, listing each book to be read within each month. This approach should help those unfamiliar with the Bible's structure to follow along more easily and ensure they cover the entire Bible in a year.

Month 1:
- Old Testament: Genesis, Exodus (up to chapter 19)
- New Testament: Matthew (up to chapter 21)

Month 2:
- Old Testament: Exodus (from chapter 20), Leviticus
- New Testament: Matthew (from chapter 22), Mark (up to chapter 9)

Month 3:
- Old Testament: Numbers, Deuteronomy (up to chapter 23)
- New Testament: Mark (from chapter 10), Luke (up to chapter 6)

Month 4:
- Old Testament: Deuteronomy (from chapter 24), Joshua
- New Testament: Luke (from chapter 7), John (up to chapter 4)

Month 5:
- Old Testament: Judges, Ruth, 1 Samuel (up to chapter 17)
- New Testament: John (from chapter 5), Acts (up to chapter 4)

Month 6:
- Old Testament: 1 Samuel (from chapter 18), 2 Samuel
- New Testament: Acts (from chapter 5), Romans (up to chapter 4)

Month 7:
- Old Testament: 1 Kings, 2 Kings (up to chapter 14)
- New Testament: Romans (from chapter 5), 1 Corinthians (up to chapter 10)

Month 8:
- Old Testament: 2 Kings (from chapter 15), 1 Chronicles, 2 Chronicles (up to chapter 9)
- New Testament: 1 Corinthians (from chapter 11), 2 Corinthians, Galatians, Ephesians

Month 9:
- Old Testament: 2 Chronicles (from chapter 10), Ezra, Nehemiah
- New Testament: Philippians, Colossians, 1 Thessalonians, 2 Thessalonians, 1 Timothy

Month 10:
- Old Testament: Esther, Job (up to chapter 7)
- New Testament: 2 Timothy, Titus, Philemon, Hebrews (up to chapter 6)

Month 11:
- Old Testament: Job (from chapter 8), Psalms (up to Psalm 55)
- New Testament: Hebrews (from chapter 7), James, 1 Peter, 2 Peter, 1 John, 2 John, 3 John, Jude, Revelation (up to chapter 11)

Month 12:
- Old Testament: Psalms (from Psalm 56), Proverbs, Ecclesiastes, Song of Solomon, Isaiah, Jeremiah, Lamentations, Ezekiel, Daniel, Hosea, Joel, Amos, Obadiah, Jonah, Micah, Nahum, Habakkuk, Zephaniah, Haggai, Zechariah, Malachi
- New Testament: Revelation (from chapter 12)

WORK THE WORD!

The Work The Word Section is a carefully curated collection of scripture designed to serve as your spiritual compass in times of need.

With life's demands, we often seek wisdom, power, and insight to navigate our paths with grace and purpose. This section is crafted to provide you with a starting point, a wellspring of divine guidance drawn directly from the Word of God.

You will find three scriptures for each topic, presented in various versions of the Bible. This diversity in translations offers a broader perspective, allowing the timeless truths of the scriptures to resonate more deeply and personally with you.

Our aim is to equip you with a spiritual toolkit, enabling you to draw upon the Word in moments of uncertainty or when in need of encouragement. These scriptures are more than just words; they are invitations to experience the transformative power of God's Word in your daily life.

As you delve into this section, may you find the wisdom, power, and insight you seek. Let these scriptures be your guide, your comfort, and your inspiration as you walk the path laid out for you, fortified by the Word and accompanied by the divine presence in every step.

Whether you're searching for encouragement, direction, or strength, these verses stand as beacons of light, illuminating your journey. **WORK THE WORD!**

FAITH AND BELIEF

1. **Hebrews 11:1** - "Now faith is confidence in what we hope for and assurance about what we do not see."
2. **Ephesians 2:8-9** - "For it is by grace you have been saved, through faith—and this is not from yourselves, it is the gift of God— not by works, so that no one can boast."
3. **Mark 11:24** - "Therefore I tell you, whatever you ask for in prayer, believe that you have received it, and it will be yours."

LOVE AND COMPASSION

1. **1 Corinthians 13:4-7** - "Love is patient, love is kind. It does not envy, it does not boast, it is not proud..."
2. **John 13:34-35** - "A new command I give you: Love one another. As I have loved you, so you must love one another."
3. **1 John 4:8** - "Whoever does not love does not know God, because God is love."

STRENGTH AND COURAGE

1. **Joshua 1:9** - "Have I not commanded you? Be strong and courageous. Do not be afraid; do not be discouraged, for the Lord your God will be with you wherever you go."
2. **Philippians 4:13** - "I can do all this through him who gives me strength."
3. **Isaiah 41:10** - "So do not fear, for I am with you; do not be dismayed, for I am your God. I will strengthen you and help you; I will uphold you with my righteous right hand."

PEACE AND COMFORT

1. **John 14:27** - "Peace I leave with you; my peace I give you. I do not give to you as the world gives. Do not let your hearts be troubled and do not be afraid."
2. **Philippians 4:6-7** - "Do not be anxious about anything, but in every situation, by prayer and petition, with thanksgiving, present your requests to God."
3. **Psalm 23:1-4** - "The Lord is my shepherd, I lack nothing..."

HOPE AND ASSURANCE

1. **Romans 15:13** - "May the God of hope fill you with all joy and peace as you trust in him, so that you may overflow with hope by the power of the Holy Spirit."
2. **Jeremiah 29:11** - "For I know the plans I have for you," declares the Lord, "plans to prosper you and not to harm you, plans to give you hope and a future."
3. **Isaiah 40:31** - "But those who hope in the Lord will renew their strength. They will soar on wings like eagles; they will run and not grow weary, they will walk and not be faint."

WISDOM AND GUIDANCE

1. **Proverbs 3:5-6** - "Trust in the Lord with all your heart and lean not on your own understanding; in all your ways submit to him, and he will make your paths straight."
2. **James 1:5** - "If any of you lacks wisdom, you should ask God, who gives generously to all without finding fault, and it will be given to you."
3. **Psalm 119:105** - "Your word is a lamp for my feet, a light on my path."

FORGIVENESS AND REDEMPTION

1. **1 John 1:9** - "If we confess our sins, he is faithful and just and will forgive us our sins and purify us from all unrighteousness."
2. **Ephesians 1:7** - "In him we have redemption through his blood, the forgiveness of sins, in accordance with the riches of God's grace."
3. **Matthew 6:14-15** - "For if you forgive other people when they sin against you, your heavenly Father will also forgive you."

SERVICE AND GIVING

1. **Matthew 25:40** - "The King will reply, 'Truly I tell you, whatever you did for one of the least of these brothers and sisters of mine, you did for me.'"
2. **Acts 20:35** - "In everything I did, I showed you that by this kind of hard work we must help the weak, remembering the words the Lord Jesus himself said: 'It is more blessed to give than to receive.'"
3. **Galatians 5:13** - "You, my brothers and sisters, were called to be free. But do not use your freedom to indulge the flesh; rather, serve one another humbly in love."

ENDURANCE AND PERSEVERANCE

1. **Romans 5:3-4** - "Not only so, but we also glory in our sufferings, because we know that suffering produces perseverance; perseverance, character; and hope."
2. **James 1:12** - "Blessed is the one who perseveres under trial because, having stood the test, that person will receive the crown of life that the Lord has promised to those who love him."
3. **Hebrews 12:1-2** - "Therefore, since we are surrounded by such a great cloud of witnesses, let us throw off everything that hinders and the sin that so easily entangles. And let us run with perseverance the race marked out for us..."

BUSINESS AND WORK

1. **Proverbs 16:3** - "Commit to the Lord whatever you do, and he will establish your plans."
2. **Colossians 3:23-24** - "Whatever you do, work at it with all your heart, as working for the Lord, not for human masters..."
3. **Proverbs 22:29** - "Do you see someone skilled in their work? They will serve before kings; they will not serve before officials of low rank."

FAMILY AND PARENTING

1. **Proverbs 22:6** - "Start children off on the way they should go, and even when they are old they will not turn from it."
2. **Ephesians 5:25** - "Husbands, love your wives, just as Christ loved the church and gave himself up for her."
3. **Ephesians 6:4** - "Fathers, do not exasperate your children; instead, bring them up in the training and instruction of the Lord."
4. **Deuteronomy 6:6-7-** "And these words, which I command thee this day, shall be in thine heart: And thou shalt teach them diligently unto thy children, and shalt talk of them when thou sittest in thine house, and when thou walkest by the way, and when thou liest down, and when thou risest up."

OVERCOMING DIFFICULT TIMES

1. **James 1:2-4** - "Consider it pure joy, my brothers and sisters, whenever you face trials of many kinds, because you know that the testing of your faith produces perseverance."
2. **Romans 8:28** - "And we know that for those who love God all things work together for good, for those who are called according to his purpose."
3. **Psalm 46:1-2** - "God is our refuge and strength, a very present help in trouble. Therefore will not we fear, though the earth be removed, and though the mountains be carried into the midst of the sea;"

LOSS AND GRIEF

1. **Matthew 5:4** - "Blessed are those who mourn, for they will be comforted."
2. **Psalm 34:18** - "The Lord is near to the brokenhearted and saves the crushed in spirit."
3. **Revelation 21:4** - "And God shall wipe away all tears from their eyes; and there shall be no more death, neither sorrow, nor crying, neither shall there be any more pain: for the former things are passed away."

HEALTH

1. **1 Corinthians 6:19-20** - "Do you not know that your bodies are temples of the Holy Spirit, who is in you, whom you have received from God? You are not your own..."
2. **3 John 1:2** - "Dear friend, I pray that you may enjoy good health and that all may go well with you, even as your soul is getting along well."
3. **Exodus 15:26** - "He said, 'If you listen carefully to the Lord your God and do what is right in his eyes, if you pay attention to his commands and keep all his decrees, I will not bring on you any of the diseases I brought on the Egyptians, for I am the Lord, who heals you.'"

HEALING

1. **James 5:14-15** - "Is anyone among you sick? Let them call the elders of the church to pray over them and anoint them with oil in the name of the Lord."
2. **Jeremiah 17:14** - "Heal me, O Lord, and I will be healed; save me and I will be saved, for you are the one I praise."
3. **Psalm 147:3** - "He heals the brokenhearted and binds up their wounds."

SALVATION

1. **Romans 10:9-10** - "If you declare with your mouth, 'Jesus is Lord,' and believe in your heart that God raised him from the dead, you will be saved."
2. **Ephesians 2:8-9** - "For it is by grace you have been saved, through faith—and this is not from yourselves, it is the gift of God— not by works, so that no one can boast."
3. **Acts 4:12** - "Salvation is found in no one else, for there is no other name under heaven given to mankind by which we must be saved."

FAITH

1. **Hebrews 11:1** - "Now faith is confidence in what we hope for and assurance about what we do not see."
2. **Ephesians 2:8-9** - "For it is by grace you have been saved, through faith—and this is not from yourselves, it is the gift of God— not by works, so that no one can boast."
3. **2 Corinthians 5:7** - "For we live by faith, not by sight."

PRAYER

1. **Philippians 4:6-7** - "Do not be anxious about anything, but in every situation, by prayer and petition, with thanksgiving, present your requests to God."
2. **1 Thessalonians 5:16-18** - "Rejoice always, pray continually, give thanks in all circumstances; for this is God's will for you in Christ Jesus."
3. **Matthew 6:6** - "But when you pray, go into your room, close the door and pray to your Father, who is unseen. Then your Father, who sees what is done in secret, will reward you."

FASTING

1. **Isaiah 58:6** - "Is not this the kind of fasting I have chosen: to loose the chains of injustice and untie the cords of the yoke, to set the oppressed free and break every yoke?"
2. **Matthew 6:17** -18 - "But when you fast, put oil on your head and wash your face, so that it will not be obvious to others that you are fasting, but only to your Father, who is unseen; and your Father, who sees what is done in secret, will reward you."
3. **Acts 13:2-3** - "While they were worshiping the Lord and fasting, the Holy Spirit said, 'Set apart for me Barnabas and Saul for the work to which I have called them.' So after they had fasted and prayed, they placed their hands on them and sent them off."

WEALTH

1. **Proverbs 10:22** - "The blessing of the Lord brings wealth, without painful toil for it."

2. **1 Timothy 6:17-19** - "Command those who are rich in this present world not to be arrogant nor to put their hope in wealth, which is so uncertain, but to put their hope in God, who richly provides us with everything for our enjoyment."

3. **Malachi 3:10** - "Bring the whole tithe into the storehouse, that there may be food in my house. Test me in this," says the Lord Almighty, "and see if I will not throw open the floodgates of heaven and pour out so much blessing that there will not be room enough to store it."

Setting Goals
VISION AND ACHIEVEMENT

Habakkuk 2:2-3

"Then the Lord replied: 'Write down the revelation and make it plain on tablets so that a herald may run with it. For the revelation awaits an appointed time; it speaks of the end and will not prove false. Though it lingers, wait for it; it will certainly come and will not delay.'"

SETTING GOALS
VISION AND ACHIEVEMENT

Prompt:

Reflect on the importance of setting goals in your life. Think about the goals you've set and achieved, and those you're still working towards. Pray for clarity in setting meaningful and achievable goals, for the determination to pursue them, and for the wisdom to align these goals with your life's purpose.

Reflection

Entrepreneurship
VISION AND GUIDANCE

Proverbs 16:3

"Commit to the Lord whatever you do, and he will establish your plans."

ENTREPRENEURSHIP
VISION AND GUIDANCE

Prompt:

Reflect on your entrepreneurial journey, the highs and lows, and the lessons learned. Consider the vision you have for your business and the impact you wish to make. Pray for guidance in your decisions, for the wisdom to lead with integrity, and for the strength to persevere through challenges. Ask for clarity in your purpose and for opportunities to grow and thrive.

Reflection

Family
UNITY AND LOVE

Colossians 3:14

"And over all these virtues put on love, which binds them all together in perfect unity."

Scripture

UNITY AND LOVE

Prompt:

Think about your family, their well-being, and the bonds you share. Reflect on the role of love, patience, and understanding in strengthening these bonds. Pray for unity within your family, for healing where there is hurt, and for love to be the foundation of all relationships. Ask for wisdom in nurturing and guiding your loved ones.

Reflection

99

I CAN DO ALL THINGS THROUGH CHRIST WHO STRENGTHENS ME.

-PHILIPPIANS 4:13

SCRIPTURE
reflection

_____

_____

_____

_____

_____

_____

_____

_____

_____

_____

_____

_____

_____

_____

_____

_____

_____

_____

_____

Healing
PHYSICAL AND EMOTIONAL

Jeremiah 17:14

"Heal me, Lord, and I will be healed; save me and I will be saved, for you are the one I praise."

HEALING
PHYSICAL AND EMOTIONAL

Prompt:

Focus on areas in your life or in the lives of those around you that need healing. Reflect on the journey of healing and the strength it requires. Pray for comfort and restoration, for patience in the healing process, and for the peace that surpasses understanding. Ask for God's healing touch in every aspect of your life.

Reflection

Faith
STRENGTHENING BELIEF

Mark 9:24

"Immediately the boy's father exclaimed, 'I do believe; help me overcome my unbelief!'"

FAITH
STRENGTHENING BELIEF

Prompt:

Contemplate your faith journey, the moments of doubt, and the times of unwavering belief. Reflect on what challenges your faith and what fortifies it. Pray for a deeper understanding of your faith, for a heart that seeks truth, and for the courage to trust even when the path is unclear. Ask for a spirit that finds joy and strength in faith.

Reflection

Wealth
RESPONSIBLE STEWARDSHIP

1 Timothy 6:17-19

"Command those who are rich in this present world not to be arrogant nor to put their hope in wealth, which is so uncertain, but to put their hope in God, who richly provides us with everything for our enjoyment."

RESPONSIBLE STEWARDSHIP

Prompt:

Reflect on your relationship with wealth and resources. Consider how you manage and utilize the blessings you've received. Pray for wisdom in stewardship, for the discernment to use resources wisely and generously, and for a heart that prioritizes people over possessions. Ask for guidance in using your wealth to make a positive difference.

Reflection

##

FOR I KNOW THE PLANS I
HAVE FOR YOU, DECLARES
THE LORD, PLANS TO
PROSPER YOU AND NOT TO
HARM YOU, PLANS TO
GIVE YOU HOPE AND A
FUTURE.

JEREMIAH 29:11

SCRIPTURE
reflection

_____

_____

_____

_____

_____

_____

_____

_____

_____

_____

_____

_____

_____

_____

_____

_____

_____

_____

_____

_____

Legacy IMPACT AND MEMORY

Proverbs 13:22

"A good person leaves an inheritance for their children's children, but a sinner's wealth is stored up for the righteous."

LEGACY
IMPACT AND MEMORY

Prompt:

Think about the legacy you want to leave behind. Reflect on the values, memories, and impact you wish to impart to the world and future generations. Pray for the ability to live a life that inspires, for the wisdom to make lasting and positive contributions, and for the foresight to build a legacy that reflects your deepest beliefs and aspirations.

Reflection

Gratitude
APPRECIATING BLESSINGS

1 Thessalonians 5:16-18

"Rejoice always, pray continually, give thanks in all circumstances; for this is God's will for you in Christ Jesus."

GRATITUDE
APPRECIATING BLESSINGS

Prompt:

Reflect on the blessings in your life, both big and small. Consider the people, opportunities, and joys that you've experienced. Pray for a heart that recognizes and appreciates these blessings, for the ability to express gratitude daily, and for the grace to see the good even in challenging times. Ask for a perspective that values thankfulness.

Reflection

Purpose
FINDING AND FULFILLING

Ephesians 2:10

"For we are God's handiwork, created in Christ Jesus
to do good works, which God prepared in advance
for us to do."

PURPOSE
FINDING AND FULFILLING

Prompt:

Contemplate your life's purpose and the paths you've taken. Reflect on your passions, talents, and the impact you desire to make. Pray for clarity in understanding your purpose, for the courage to pursue it wholeheartedly, and for the perseverance to continue even when obstacles arise. Ask for opportunities to use your gifts in meaningful ways.

Reflection

"

SO DO NOT FEAR, FOR I AM WITH YOU; DO NOT BE DISMAYED, FOR I AM YOUR GOD. I WILL STRENGTHEN YOU AND HELP YOU; I WILL UPHOLD YOU WITH MY RIGHTEOUS RIGHT HAND.

ISAIAH 41:10

SCRIPTURE reflection

_____
_____
_____
_____
_____
_____
_____
_____
_____
_____
_____
_____
_____
_____
_____
_____
_____
_____
_____
_____
_____

Business Growth
INNOVATION AND ADAPTABILITY

Isaiah 43:19

"See, I am doing a new thing! Now it springs up; do you not perceive it? I am making a way in the wilderness and streams in the wasteland."

BUSINESS GROWTH
INNOVATION AND ADAPTABILITY

Prompt:

Reflect on the growth journey of your business. Think about the innovations you've implemented and the adaptability you've shown in the face of change. Pray for continued creativity, the foresight to anticipate market changes, and the agility to adapt your business strategies effectively.

Reflection

Forgiveness
LETTING GO AND HEALING

Matthew 6:14-15

"For if you forgive other people when they sin against you, your heavenly Father will also forgive you."

LETTING GO AND HEALING

Prompt:

Think about the areas in your life where forgiveness is needed. This could be forgiving others or seeking forgiveness for yourself. Reflect on the power of forgiveness in healing and restoring relationships. Pray for the strength to forgive, for the humility to seek forgiveness, and for the wisdom to understand the freedom that comes with letting go of resentment and anger.

Reflection

Courage
FACING FEARS AND TAKING RISKS

Joshua 1:9

"Have I not commanded you? Be strong and courageous. Do not be afraid; do not be discouraged, for the Lord your God will be with you wherever you go."

COURAGE
FACING FEARS AND TAKING RISKS

Prompt:

Reflect on the fears and uncertainties that hold you back.
Consider the risks you need to take to grow and achieve your
goals. Pray for the courage to face your fears, for the boldness
to step out of your comfort zone, and for the confidence to trust
in your abilities and in God's plan. Ask for the bravery to take
calculated risks that lead to growth.

Reflection

"

GOD IS OUR REFUGE AND STRENGTH, AN EVER-PRESENT HELP IN TROUBLE."

PSALM 46:1

SCRIPTURE
reflection

_____

_____

_____

_____

_____

_____

_____

_____

_____

_____

_____

_____

_____

_____

_____

_____

_____

_____

_____

Peace
INNER CALM AND HARMONY

Philippians 4:6-7

"Do not be anxious about anything, but in every situation, by prayer and petition, with thanksgiving, present your requests to God. And the peace of God, which transcends all understanding, will guard your hearts and your minds in Christ Jesus."

PEACE
INNER CALM AND HARMONY

Prompt:

Think about the aspects of your life where you seek peace.
Reflect on the internal and external conflicts you face. Pray for
inner calm in the midst of chaos, for harmony in your
relationships, and for the wisdom to create environments of
peace around you. Ask for the ability to be a peacemaker and
for the serenity that comes from trusting in a higher plan.

Reflection

Wisdom
INSIGHT AND UNDERSTANDING

James 1:5

"If any of you lacks wisdom, you should ask God, who gives generously to all without finding fault, and it will be given to you."

WISDOM
INSIGHT AND UNDERSTANDING

Prompt:

Consider the decisions and choices you face in life. Reflect on the need for wisdom in navigating these choices. Pray for insight and understanding in all aspects of your life, for the discernment to make wise decisions, and for the humility to seek guidance and learn from others. Ask for wisdom that is rooted in love, compassion, and justice.

Reflection

Hope
OPTIMISM AND EXPECTATION

Romans 15:13

"May the God of hope fill you with all joy and peace as you trust in him, so that you may overflow with hope by the power of the Holy Spirit."

HOPE
OPTIMISM AND EXPECTATION

Prompt:

Reflect on the role of hope in your life. Consider the times when hope has guided you through difficult moments. Pray for an enduring sense of optimism, for the ability to see the light even in the darkest times, and for the expectation of good things to come. Ask for a heart that holds onto hope, even when circumstances are challenging.

Reflection

99

COME TO ME, ALL YOU WHO ARE WEARY AND BURDENED, AND I WILL GIVE YOU REST.

MATTHEW 11:28

SCRIPTURE
reflection

_____

_____

_____

_____

_____

_____

_____

_____

_____

_____

_____

_____

_____

_____

_____

_____

_____

_____

_____

Patience
ENDURANCE AND PERSEVERANCE

James 5:7-8

"Be patient, then, brothers and sisters, until the Lord's coming. See how the farmer waits for the land to yield its valuable crop, patiently waiting for the autumn and spring rains."

PATIENCE
ENDURANCE AND PERSEVERANCE

Prompt:

Think about the situations where you need patience. Reflect on the challenges that test your endurance and the goals that require perseverance. Pray for the strength to wait with grace, for the endurance to persevere through trials, and for the wisdom to understand the value of patience in achieving long-term success. Ask for a spirit that embraces patience as a virtue.

Reflection

Compassion
EMPATHY AND KINDNESS

Colossians 3:12

"Therefore, as God's chosen people, holy and dearly loved, clothe yourselves with compassion, kindness, humility, gentleness and patience."

Scripture

COMPASSION
EMPATHY AND KINDNESS

Prompt:

Reflect on the importance of compassion in your life. Consider how empathy and kindness have impacted you and how you can extend them to others. Pray for a heart that feels deeply for others, for the eyes to see the needs around you, and for the hands to offer help and kindness. Ask for the ability to walk in others' shoes and to act with genuine compassion.

Reflection

Integrity
HONESTY AND MORAL COURAGE

Proverbs 10:9

"Whoever walks in integrity walks securely, but whoever takes crooked paths will be found out."

HONESTY AND MORAL COURAGE

Prompt:

Think about the role of integrity in your personal and professional life. Reflect on the times you've had to stand up for what is right, even when it was difficult. Pray for the courage to always act with honesty and moral fortitude, for the strength to uphold your values, and for the wisdom to discern right from wrong. Ask for a character that reflects integrity in every aspect of your life.

Reflection

"

AND WE KNOW THAT IN ALL THINGS GOD WORKS FOR THE GOOD OF THOSE WHO LOVE HIM, WHO HAVE BEEN CALLED ACCORDING TO HIS PURPOSE.

MATTHEW 11:28

SCRIPTURE reflection

_____

_____

_____

_____

_____

_____

_____

_____

_____

_____

_____

_____

_____

_____

_____

_____

_____

_____

_____

Service
GIVING BACK AND HELPING OTHERS

Galatians 5:13

"You, my brothers and sisters, were called to be free.
But do not use your freedom to indulge the flesh;
rather, serve one another humbly in love."

SERVICE
GIVING BACK AND HELPING OTHERS

Prompt:

Consider the ways you can serve and give back to your community and the world. Reflect on the joy and fulfillment that come from helping others. Pray for opportunities to serve, for the heart to see the needs of others, and for the resources and abilities to make a positive impact. Ask for a life that is marked by selfless service and generosity.

Reflection

Contentment
SATISFACTION AND FULFILLMENT

Philippians 4:11-12

"I am not saying this because I am in need, for I have learned to be content whatever the circumstances."

CONTENTMENT
SATISFACTION AND FULFILLMENT

Prompt:

Reflect on your journey towards contentment. Consider what true satisfaction and fulfillment mean to you. Pray for the ability to find contentment in your current circumstances, for the wisdom to distinguish between needs and wants, and for the peace that comes from a grateful heart. Ask for the strength to find joy in simplicity and fulfillment in the present moment.

Reflection

Humility
MODESTY AND SELF-REFLECTION

Proverbs 22:4

"Humility is the fear of the Lord; its wages are riches and honor and life."

Scripture

MODESTY AND SELF-REFLECTION

Prompt:

Think about the role of humility in your life. Reflect on the importance of staying grounded and the value of self-reflection. Pray for a humble spirit, for the ability to recognize your own strengths and weaknesses, and for the grace to learn from others. Ask for the wisdom to lead with humility and to always remember the source of your blessings.

Reflection

"

HAVE I NOT COMMANDED YOU? BE STRONG AND COURAGEOUS. DO NOT BE AFRAID; DO NOT BE DISCOURAGED, FOR THE LORD YOUR GOD WILL BE WITH YOU WHEREVER YOU GO.

JOSHUA 1:9

SCRIPTURE *reflection*

_____

_____

_____

_____

_____

_____

_____

_____

_____

_____

_____

_____

_____

_____

_____

_____

_____

_____

_____

_____

_____

Generosity
SHARING AND GIVING

2 Corinthians 9:6-7

"Remember this: Whoever sows sparingly will also reap sparingly, and whoever sows generously will also reap generously. Each of you should give what you have decided in your heart to give, not reluctantly or under compulsion, for God loves a cheerful giver."

GENEROSITY
SHARING AND GIVING

Prompt:

Consider how generosity has played a role in your life. Reflect on the joy of giving and the impact it has on both the giver and the receiver. Pray for a generous heart, for the willingness to share your resources, time, and talents, and for the discernment to give wisely. Ask for the joy that comes from selfless giving and the ability to bless others through your generosity.

Reflection

Joy
HAPPINESS AND DELIGHT

Nehemiah 8:10

"Do not grieve, for the joy of the Lord is your strength."

JOY
HAPPINESS AND DELIGHT

Prompt:

Reflect on the sources of joy in your life. Consider the moments that bring you happiness and the things that fill you with delight. Pray for an ever-present sense of joy, for the ability to find happiness in the simple things, and for a spirit that radiates positivity. Ask for the grace to spread joy to those around you and to always find reasons to smile.

Reflection

Discernment
MAKING WISE CHOICES

Proverbs 3:5-6

"Trust in the Lord with all your heart and lean not on
your own understanding; in all your ways submit to
him, and he will make your paths straight."

DISCERNMENT
MAKING WISE CHOICES

Prompt:

Think about the decisions you face in your life. Reflect on the importance of discernment in making wise choices. Pray for clarity in decision-making, for the insight to understand the implications of your choices, and for the wisdom to choose paths that align with your values and goals. Ask for the discernment to distinguish between what is good and what is best.

Reflection

99

BUT HE SAID TO ME, 'MY GRACE IS SUFFICIENT FOR YOU, FOR MY POWER IS MADE PERFECT IN WEAKNESS.' THEREFORE I WILL BOAST ALL THE MORE GLADLY ABOUT MY WEAKNESSES, SO THAT CHRIST'S POWER MAY REST ON ME.

2 CORINTHIANS 12:9

SCRIPTURE reflection

_____

_____

_____

_____

_____

_____

_____

_____

_____

_____

_____

_____

_____

_____

_____

_____

_____

_____

_____

_____

Perseverance
ENDURING AND OVERCOMING

Romans 5:3-4

"Not only so, but we also glory in our sufferings, because we know that suffering produces perseverance; perseverance, character; and character, hope."

PERSEVERANCE
ENDURING AND OVERCOMING

Prompt:

Consider the challenges and obstacles you've faced and overcome. Reflect on the importance of perseverance in achieving your goals. Pray for the endurance to keep going even when the journey is tough, for the strength to overcome setbacks, and for the faith to believe that every effort is worth it. Ask for the perseverance to pursue your dreams relentlessly.

Reflection

Kindness
COMPASSION AND GENTLENESS

Colossians 3:12

"Therefore, as God's chosen people, holy and dearly loved, clothe yourselves with compassion, kindness, humility, gentleness and patience."

KINDNESS
COMPASSION AND GENTLENESS

Prompt:

Reflect on the moments when kindness touched your life or when you extended kindness to others. Think about the profound impact that compassionate words and gentle actions can have. Pray for a heart that naturally inclines towards kindness, for the sensitivity to perceive the needs of those around you, and for the grace to respond with compassion and gentleness. Ask for the strength to be a beacon of kindness in a world that often feels harsh and uncaring, and for the wisdom to understand that every act of kindness, no matter how small, can make a significant difference.

Reflection

Personal Development
SELF-IMPROVEMENT AND LEARNING

Philippians 1:6

"Being confident of this, that he who began a good work in you will carry it on to completion until the day of Christ Jesus."

PERSONAL DEVELOPMENT
SELF-IMPROVEMENT AND LEARNING

Prompt:

Contemplate your journey of personal development. Reflect on the areas where you've grown and the aspects of yourself you're still exploring. Pray for self-awareness, the discipline for self-improvement, and the wisdom to embrace your unique path of growth.

Reflection

"

EVEN THOUGH I WALK THROUGH THE DARKEST VALLEY, I WILL FEAR NO EVIL, FOR YOU ARE WITH ME; YOUR ROD AND YOUR STAFF, THEY COMFORT ME.

PSALM 23:4

SCRIPTURE *reflection*

Mental Health
PEACE AND BALANCE

2 Timothy 1:7

"For God has not given us a spirit of fear, but of power and of love and of a sound mind."

MENTAL HEALTH
PEACE AND BALANCE

Prompt:

Think about the state of your mental health and well-being.
Reflect on the practices that contribute to your peace of mind
and emotional balance. Pray for mental resilience, the strength to
seek help when needed, and for a supportive community that
understands and uplifts you.

Reflection

Perseverance in Hard Times
STRENGTH AND ENDURANCE

Romans 5:3-4

> "Not only so, but we also glory in our sufferings, because we know that suffering produces perseverance; perseverance, character; and character, hope."

PERSEVERANCE IN HARD TIMES
STRENGTH AND ENDURANCE

Prompt:

Consider the difficult times you've faced and how you've managed to persevere through them. Reflect on the sources of your strength and endurance during these challenges. Pray for the resilience to push through when times are hard, for the courage to face adversity, and for the faith to know that these trials are shaping you for the better.

Reflection

Embracing Change
ADAPTABILITY AND GROWTH

Isaiah 43:19

"See, I am doing a new thing! Now it springs up; do you not perceive it? I am making a way in the wilderness and streams in the wasteland."

EMBRACING CHANGE
ADAPTABILITY AND GROWTH

Prompt:

Think about the changes you've experienced in your life, both expected and unexpected. Reflect on how you've adapted to these changes. Pray for the flexibility to embrace change, for the openness to grow through new experiences, and for the trust in God's plan through all seasons of life.

Reflection

Living Fully
JOY AND PRESENCE

John 10:10

"The thief comes only to steal and kill and destroy; I came that they may have life, and have it abundantly."

LIVING FULLY
JOY AND PRESENCE

Prompt:

Reflect on what it means to live fully in each moment. Consider the ways you can embrace life more fully, with joy and presence. Pray for the ability to appreciate life's simple pleasures, for the mindfulness to be fully present in each moment, and for the courage to live life to its fullest potential.

Reflection

"

TRUST IN THE LORD WITH ALL YOUR HEART AND LEAN NOT ON YOUR OWN UNDERSTANDING; IN ALL YOUR WAYS SUBMIT TO HIM, AND HE WILL MAKE YOUR PATHS STRAIGHT.

PROVERBS 3:5-6

SCRIPTURE reflection

_____

_____

_____

_____

_____

_____

_____

_____

_____

_____

_____

_____

_____

_____

_____

_____

_____

_____

_____

_____

_____

_____

_____

PRAYER
notes

_____
_____
_____
_____
_____
_____
_____
_____
_____
_____
_____
_____
_____
_____
_____
_____
_____
_____
_____

GOD STILL *speaks*

_____

_____

_____

_____

_____

_____

_____

_____

_____

_____

_____

_____

_____

_____

_____

_____

_____

_____

_____

PRAYER
notes

_____
_____
_____
_____
_____
_____
_____
_____
_____
_____
_____
_____
_____
_____
_____
_____
_____
_____
_____
_____
_____

GOD STILL *speaks*

_____

_____

_____

_____

_____

_____

_____

_____

_____

_____

_____

_____

_____

_____

_____

_____

_____

_____

_____

PRAYER
notes

_____
_____
_____
_____
_____
_____
_____
_____
_____
_____
_____
_____
_____
_____
_____
_____
_____
_____
_____
_____

GOD STILL *speaks*

_____

_____

_____

_____

_____

_____

_____

_____

_____

_____

_____

_____

_____

_____

_____

_____

_____

_____

PRAYER
notes

_____

_____

_____

_____

_____

_____

_____

_____

_____

_____

_____

_____

_____

_____

_____

_____

_____

_____

_____

_____

GOD STILL *speaks*

_____

_____

_____

_____

_____

_____

_____

_____

_____

_____

_____

_____

_____

_____

_____

_____

_____

_____

_____

_____

_____

_____

PRAYER
notes

_____
_____
_____
_____
_____
_____
_____
_____
_____
_____
_____
_____
_____
_____
_____
_____
_____
_____
_____
_____
_____

GOD STILL
speaks!

_____

_____

_____

_____

_____

_____

_____

_____

_____

_____

_____

_____

_____

_____

_____

_____

_____

_____

Made in the USA
Monee, IL
04 April 2024

55730888R00066